SEVEN DAYS IN NICARAGUA LIBRE

Lawrence Ferlinghetti

Photographs by Chris Felver

City Lights Books
San Francisco

Cover: Painting by Miriam Guevara: *El Algodonal.*
Courtesy of Ministerio de Cultura Managua, Nicaragua

Ferlinghetti, Lawrence.
    Seven days in Nicaragua libre.

    Bibliography: p.
    1. Ferlinghetti, Lawrence—Diaries. 2. Ferlinghetti,
Lawrence—Journeys—Nicaragua. 3. Poets, American—20th
century—Biography. 4. Nicaragua—Description and
travel—1951- . 5. Nicaragua—Politics and government
—1979- . I. Title. II. Title: 7 days in Nicaragua
libre.
PS3511.E557Z476 1984   811'.54 [B]   84—19871
ISBN 0-87286-160-0 (pbk.)

CITY LIGHTS BOOKS are edited by Lawrence Ferlinghetti & Nancy J. Peters
and published at the City Lights Bookstore, 261 Columbus Avenue, San
Francisco, California 94133.

SEVEN DAYS IN NICARAGUA LIBRE

I went to Nicaragua in the last week of January, 1984, to give the poet and Minister of Culture, Father Ernesto Cardenal, a seed from a flower at Boris Pasternak's grave which had been given to me by the Russian poet Andrei Voznesenski at a poetry reading against war at UNESCO in Paris.

When I presented the seed to Cardenal in an open-air amphitheater in Managua, I felt I did not have to point out to him nor the audience that the seed was a symbol not only of the power of poetry to transcend all the boundaries of the world dividing people from each other, but also a symbol (from the grave of that great Russian writer who survived the most repressive period of Soviet life) of resistance to Stalinism. The theater was in the Plaza Pedro Joaquin Chamorro, who was murdered near the end of Somoza's dictatorship, the outrage over it in fact hastening the end of the regime.

I also went to Nicaragua to deliver the first copies of a City Lights anthology of Central American poetry, *Volcán,* and to see the Sandinist revolution for myself.

As a civil libertarian tourist of revolution, I hoped at least to probe the supposed limits of what one anarchist member of the Sailors Union of the Pacific in San Francisco had called "Potemkin Village Tours."

I came to Nicaragua thinking that what was happening here was not, in fact, a revolution, not at least in the sense of the dreamed ideal of many intellectual revolutionaries, particularly anarchists. What has happened here, rather, is the overthrow of a tyrant (Somoza) supported by the U.S., and the attempt to overthrow the economic tyrant of colonialism in which Latin America has been for centuries the cheap labor market for North American and multinational business. It is not so much a revolution as it is a crisis of decolonization in a poor country the size of the San Francisco Bay Area in population, devastated by U.S.-financed war, desperately short of supplies, attempting to set up some sort of "democratic" government (in the teeth of a U.S. policy evidently designed to force Nicaragua into the Soviet camp and thus give the U.S. justification to move in and "control" the situation.)

In the face of all this, were the Sandinistas now setting up a Soviet-style authoritarian government? As a civil libertarian with anarchist sympathies, I was interested in discovering just how much "authority" is absolutely needed to lift a country out of colonialism into a free society. Was it possible at all, without losing the very freedom revolutionists always proclaim? The answer to that question is the history of revolutions.

Nicaragua is now the focus of passions of the Left, fifty years after such passion and hope were concentrated in Republican Spain—and disappointed; twenty-five years after the same hopes were concentrated on Cuba. Everyone dreams their ideal of a perfect society—and are disappointed or disillusioned. The absolute is unobtainable.

In the history of revolutions, the issue of individual civil rights and especially freedom of speech and press has been the pivot upon which all in the end has stood or fallen. So it was in Cuba—to the dismay of many early supporters; so it will be in Nicaragua—whose leaders are trying valiantly, it would seem, to avoid the mistakes Cuba made.

How *libre* would "libre" turn out to be?

January 27——I'm making the trip with Chris Felver, the San Francisco photographer known for his studies of poets and for his film on the Beat Generation shown recently on television. On Aeronica Flight 500 from Miami, we seem to be the only North Americans, except for one 22-year-old student with backpack going to work two weeks with other volunteers in the coffee harvest. The plane flew directly over the eastern end of Cuba. Suddenly, after some two and a half hours, we are over the dark green waters of Lake Managua, circling down into the heart of this Caribbean amphitheatre where the fate of Central America is being played out.

The stewardess makes her announcement, first in Spanish, then English; the fifty passengers stir—mostly well-dressed Nicaraguans looking like they've been shopping in Miami—one lady shrugging and saying there's nothing to buy in Managua, and that the only reason she's going back is because she has a big house there. It wasn't taken away from her by the Sandinistas, but she says she'll lose it if she stays away more than six months. She had members of her family on both sides. It wasn't wise to take sides. Her heavy rings glittered. (Later we were to have a guide in her early twenties, recently returned from student years abroad where her family had sent her when the revolution started, who looked like she might have been a daughter of this woman.) The plane lets down its landing gear with a thump, and then we are coming in low over the brown-green fields, over farmland with brown and white houses, stone or adobe. The first impression is how small everything is—the whole of Managua seen at a glimpse in the falling sun, the center of it flattened by the earthquake of 1972 and still to be rebuilt—the whole town seeming about the size of Mazatlan or Guadalajara years ago—the airport tiny. (As an old Mexico hand, I find myself falling back on these comparisons.)

Ernesto Cardenal is there on the apron of the field, waiting to greet us, wearing a black beret and a white *cotóna*, or short-sleeved blouse, and blue jeans. The plane doors open and we file down—handshakes and *abrazos*, Ernesto beaming, with that angelic smile of his, his head as always slightly cocked to one side. It is as if I'd known him forever, though I'd met him only once before the Revolution and once since in San Francisco, and hadn't known him at Columbia University or later when he was Thomas Merton's disciple at the Trappist monastery in Gethsemane, Kentucky. Now in his late fifties, there seemed to be something childlike and eternal about him; but perhaps all small older men with white beards have that effect. (He guards his inner self, as all public holy men must. There is still enough of a Trappist in him to preserve him even in a revolution. He also guards the inner Revolution, and you don't get much out of him on any dissident subject, at least if you are a journalist.)

Walking to the airport building, I note one big camouflage-colored copter with two guards in fatigues with AK-47's guarding it. There aren't any other planes in sight, military or commercial. (Their commercial air force seems to consist of no more than four planes—two in the service to Miami, two to Mexico City. I have a feeling that "security" is definitely tight—a lot of uniforms in sight, but hardly a state of war.) We are escorted into an upstairs V.I.P. lounge in the two-story white building. A waiter in a white coat is circulating with demitasses of black coffee on a tray, a napkin on his arm. One would think it's the old days; but it isn't. Two Nicaraguan journalists sit down to interview me, one from *El Diario*, the other from the Sandinista radio station. "Why have you come?" An excellent question. I see it as a voyage of discovery, hoping to discover the Sandinistas are in the right, and that I might take some public stand in their favor, rather than the political silence maintained by many U.S. writers today. (Not exactly with that much-vaunted objectivity of North American journalists, I hope I at least have an open mind, but a mind not so open that the brains fall out.) I also tell the journalists I hope to make some new breach in the wall of enormous ignorance and misinformation and indifference in the U.S. on the subject of the Sandinist government and Nicaragua in general.

(As I write this, a story appears in *The New York Times* by Francis X. Clines entitled "Propaganda, Propagation or Just Prop," with the following lead: "Washington, June 14—White House officials scoffed when a reporter asked whether they might be running a ministry of propaganda. But a little-noticed White House 'outreach' program has been working steadily for a year now at disseminating the Reagan Administration's view that Nicaragua is a Communist beachhead threatening the hemisphere and that the American public is not being fully informed of the danger." The story goes on to outline the extensive activities of this "White House Outreach Working Group" and mentions particularly its attempts to rebut the recently reported contention of David C. MacMichael, a former Central Intelligence Agency analyst, that the Reagan Administration has been misleading Congress and the public about Nicaragua. On June 18, the *Times* printed an editorial with the following quote from MacMichael, accusing the Administration of "systematically misrepresenting Nicaraguan involvement in the supply of arms to Salvadoran guerrillas to justify its efforts to overthrow the Nicaraguan government.")

The interviews take about 20 minutes, by which time we are checked through their Customs and Immigration, and our passports returned to us.

We meet Bill Finnegan, from *New Age* magazine (Boston) and Ken Silverman, photographer for Finnegan and stringer for the *New York Times*, both of whom will be traveling with us a good deal. Finnegan tells us that downstairs in the airport, where the general public goes through, it took them over two hours, sweating with no air conditioning. Up here it's cool. There's a senator from India being interviewed in another corner. (It is Doctor Shri Shyam Sunder Mohapatra, and a story later in *La Barricada* quotes the senator as expressing "the preoccupations of his government with the way the U.S. tries to undermine the

Coming in from the airport, Managua, the brave signs greet us . . .

SANDINO

1927 1934

Yo no estoy dispuesto a entregar mis armas
en caso de que todos lo hagan. Yo me haré
morir con los pocos que me acompañan porque es preferible hacernos morir como rebeldes y no vivir como esclavos.

A. C. Sandino
(Yalí, 27 de mayo de 1927)

"better to die rebels than live as slaves . . . "

independence of Central American and Caribbean countries" and saying that "it doesn't look good for North American democracy when such a powerful country supports the military dictators of the area." He also said India was sending medical aid to Nicaragua and helping in the construction of railroads, as well as other technical industrial help. Nicaragua, he said, could count on India for support as part of the Movement of Non-Aligned Countries, of which India is the President.)

We're soon out of the airport and on the road to town in a standard Toyota sedan (no bullet-proof glass?) We're on a newly-paved road, behind us a jeep with soldiers pointing their automatics at everyone, Ernesto pointing out the great empty spaces of the city devastated by the earthquake over a decade ago, and then the great park created by the Sandinistas out of that waste in the center of Managua. What's left of the "business district" looks at first glance like downtown Salinas, California, fifty years ago—one highrise on a hill is the pyramid-like Hotel Intercontinental (where the few tourists and most foreign journalists stay). Our little cavalcade pulls up another hill overlooking the center of town, and we get out in front of the government guest house. The neighborhood has the feel of a rich suburb in any Latin American city. Only in one of those posh suburbs there wouldn't be a big poster painted on a wall across the street with a quote addressed to Carlos Fonseca (one founder of the Sandinista Liberation Front) which can be translated as "Carlos, dawn is no longer a fantasy in our

"Dawn is no longer a fantasy in our minds but a reality"

minds but a reality." (The quote is from Tomás Borge, Sandinista Minister of the Interior—it's the title for one of his books on the Revolution.)

We're installed in a mansion formerly owned by *Somocistas*. I am one of a succession of international writers invited to the continuing Festival Rubén Darío, but it happens we are the only guests here this week. There are two empty swimming pools. We sit down on a tiled veranda in the shade, and are served by a houseboy in a white coat—Tonya beer in mugs. Ernesto looks through our new anthology, *Volcán*. We rock in big wooden chairs . . .

The poet Daisy Zamora

January 28th——Wake at six to the sound of a bird I've never heard before—a macaw of some kind. I go out in the stillness of the early light and walk around the veranda and walled gardens. Next to the first swimming pool, an old old guardian sits, silent, staring into the still water. I wonder if he was sitting like that back when this was one of Somoza's henchmen's houses . . .

The bougainvillea are in bloom in Managua, in a garden across the street, as they were in the first sentence of the photo book *Nicaragua: the War of Liberation* by Richard Cross, the American photo-journalist killed last year at the Honduran Front . . .

At nine, Daisy Zamora shows up as scheduled to take us to the Museum of the Armed Forces. Daisy Zamora is one of the Nicaraguan poets in the City Lights anthology, and her latest book is *La Violenta Espuma*. She told us parts of her story. When her husband was preparing to join a surprise attack on a post of Somoza's National Guard, one night at the beginning of the Sandinista victory, she insisted on going with him, though she'd never fired a gun. He taught her how to use one. There were twelve of them with small arms, against a garrison with heavy weapons. When the surprise attack started in the darkness, she felt a "terrible loneliness," realizing that she had no one else to depend on, and had to survive on her own. They were surrounded, but they made it through and took the barracks.

A homemade tank

Somoza's horse

She said her story was typical of many young Nicaraguan women. Over 30 percent of the Sandinist fighters were women. They fought alongside the men, they were all in the streets at the time the Sandinist victory swept the country. (Women fought in greater numbers than in the Cuban revolution a decade earlier.) They felt that in the fighting they had won equal rights with the men, rights which she felt women were still fighting for in the U.S. Until recently, when Daisy Zamora had to take a less demanding job, she was Assistant Minister of Culture. (Speaking of billboards, I later noticed that there are none showing women's bodies to sell products—the Sandinistas passed a law prohibiting the use of sexist advertising.)

Outside the Museum of the Armed Forces—a single-story building like a gym—a lot of relics of the Sandinist victory are set up. Dominating it is a monumental statue of the dictator, Anastasio Somoza Garcia, on horseback. It lies where it was toppled over by the Sandinistas on the day of liberation, 19 July 1979. It is as if you could still hear its snorting, as the dust settled in the swirling wind of history.

There is also on display a rusty home-made tank about the size of a VW bug. There are some little mortars made of stove pipes. Inside, there is a kind of school bulletin board display of the history of the Sandinistas, with many photos of early heroes—Agosto Sandino, Carlos Fonseca, and others perished earlier, as well as heroes and martyrs of the final victory. There is a photo of poet Rigoberto Lopez Perez who killed the *first* Somoza at a party in 1956 in León, Nicaragua, disguised as a waiter. He was immediately killed and his body destroyed.

ANSIEDAD

YO ESTOY SUFRIENDO.
YO TENGO EL DOLOR DE TODA MI PATRIA,
Y EN MIS VENAS ANDA UN HEROE BUSCANDO LIBERTAD.

LAS FLORES DE MIS DIAS SIEMPRE ESTARAN MARCHITAS
SI LA SANGRE DEL TIRANO ESTA EN SUS VENAS.

YO ESTOY BUSCANDO EL PEZ DE LA LIBERTAD
EN LA MUERTE DEL TIRANO.

RIGOBERTO LOPEZ PEREZ

LEON, NICARAGUA, 1956

En esta forma quedó el compañero Rigoberto López
Pérez, con 35 perforaciones de bala de todos
los calibres.

Después de muerto se ensañaron con el cuerpo,
lo patearon, lo manosearon, en la flácara frente al
Teatro González y en la acera lo dejaron hasta el
22 de Septiembre. En la actualidad nadie sabe
donde quedó el compañero; Rigoberto.

The poet and his poem ...

But they did not kill his poetry. Next to his photo is a poem, *"Ansiedad."* A rough translation:

ANXIETY

I'm suffering
And I share the suffering of all my country
And in my mind
There is a hero
Looking for liberty
The flower of all my days
Will always stay faded
As long as the tyrant's blood
Remains in his veins
I'm looking for the fish of liberty
in the blood of his death

On the way back across town, we drive by the new Parque Central and the amphitheater where I'll read poetry with Cardenal a few days later. We pass the Palacio Nacional and the Catholic cathedral, both heavily damaged by the earthquake of 1973 and never restored. It was as if the earthquake itself were the first great blow against the dictator. It is symbolic that the upper hierarchy of the Church—

divided in its ranks against the Sandinistas—doesn't want the towers of the cathedral torn down, though they are dangerously faulted and unrepairable.

We stop for a beer at a wooden pavilion on the edge of a *laguna*, a lake in a crater about the size of a football field. At a cantina by the water, we watch kids running and diving and sunning themselves. The noon sun beats down. It is almost as if we were at some peacetime tropical resort. "Up there," points Daisy, "just over that hill, was one of Somoza's villas. People couldn't swim here then."

Speaking of tropical resorts, we are going to one after lunch—Pochomil, on the Pacific coast. It's Saturday, and Ernesto is glad to get out of town—he hasn't been away from his work in weeks. He comes and gets us in his sedan with the soldier-driver. Ken Silverman and Bill Finnegan are in a jeep behind us, and there's another jeep with soldiers bringing up the rear. It's a little more than an hour west to the beach. Small farms and rolling land. Cows and dogs in their eternal present watch the past and the future roll by (in the form of ourselves), the cows munching their cuds and staring, the dogs standing still and barking at the Revolution. They are a little like the bourgeois lady on the plane—ready for anything, they will survive. Dawn is long past, and the sun stands at the meridian. We hope there will be no death in the afternoon.

We roll into Pochomil and the tiny beach resort built since the Revolution—a few thatched-roof beach houses and an open-air restaurant and bar facing out onto the wide beach and sea. A few *palapas* and outbuildings strung along the ocean front, set

At the resort in the laguna

back under the palms. It's like an unspoiled Mexico before the tourists arrived with their various kinds of pollution, cultural and otherwise. Fishermen and *campesinos* come up and happily greet Ernesto. We sit down at a table under an arbor. Michael Jackson and Paul McCartney blare from jukeboxes. We are soon furnished with *camarones* and *mariscos* and Tonya beer. Ernesto has some clear rum. I've never seen him without his beret before. He's not bald; he's got white hair almost to his shoulders.

Ernesto says someday they'll have tourists, someday this resort will be built up, avoiding the pollution of prostitution and the other forms of *usura* which were so much a part of Batista's Cuba and Somoza's Nicaragua. When your country is an economic slave to Rome, the Romans come, and it is your women that bleed the most. (See Eduardo Galeano's *Open Veins of Latin America*.) Ernesto's use of the Latin word for usury reminds me that Ezra Pound was one of his poetic masters.

Ernesto has another rum. He would like to kick back and relax; but the journalists bore in with their hard questions. It goes on for hours. He answers them steadily, he never seems to tire. There is a sweetness about him, almost angelic, mixed with a touch of Cupid . . . *Temperance and fortitude*, he insists (echoing Carlos Fonseca), are the distinguishing characteristics of this Revolution and of the *junta* directing it. *Junta*, he points out, doesn't mean a military dictatorship; the dictionary simply says it's a "group." The Revolution is being directed by a group—there is no single dictator, no dictatorship except of "the people." (I'd heard that before—in Havana in 1960-61—in the early euphoric stages of the Cuban Revolution, before their revolution became institutionalized—or sovietized. Ernesto is only the first of the government leaders to tell me they are trying to avoid the mistakes the Cubans made—as Fidel Castro himself counseled them to. Castro was in fact quoted in *La Prensa* as saying, "I am not a follower of Moscow; I am its victim.") And Ernesto went on to say that the Sandinist model for the Revolution is neither the Cuban nor the Soviet, and that for himself as a priest the model is the kingdom of God. And with his vision of a primitive Christianity, it was logical for him to add that in his view the Revolution would not have succeeded until there were no more masters and no more slaves. "The Gospels," he said, "foresee a classless society. They foresee also *the withering away of the state.*"

The sun is falling into the ocean, like a great round sun stone, whirling, the Aztec calendar stone, a roulette wheel in time. We walk along the long beach, our figures casting long shadows, like Giacometti statues, gesturing against the darkening sky, in the soft glowing dusk. The sun of a sudden turns dark red as it sinks in the ocean. Caught in clouds on the far horizon, it becomes a great ship afire—Turner's burning slave ship—and blood "incarnadines the multitudinous sea."

Earlier this season, the ships and port of Corinto on this coast were set afire by *contras* financed by the CIA, that international terrorist group.

Children at Pochomil

Poets on a Sunday outing. Front row (L to R): the Mexican poet Juan Bañuelos; Father Ernesto Cardenal; Nicaraguan poet and pediatrician Fernando Silva; LF. Back row: Julio Valle, editor and poet; Luis Rocha, winner of the Premio Rubén Darío.

January 29——At nine in the morning a group of writers shows up with Ernesto for the day's excursion. There's the poet Juan Bañuelos from Mexico whom I'd met at a poetry festival in Mexico D.F. two summers ago. There's Julio Valle, an editor and poet. There's Fernando Silva—a poet who is a pediatrician in charge of a clinic in Managua. Ernesto calls him "the William Carlos Williams of Nicaragua." There's Luis Rocha, winner of 1983 Premio Rubén Darío (for his poetry book, *Phocas*) and editor of the literary supplement to *El Nuevo Diario*, whose staff is partly made up of writers who resigned from *La Prensa* after the Sandinist victory. There's Luz Marina Acosta, a young poet and assistant to the Minister of Culture. She's learning English.

After a coffee, we take off for Masaya and Monimbó, the place where resistance to Somoza's National Guard was fiercest. It's just a few miles west of Managua. At its edge there's a rough wood sign:

AQUI
COMIENZA
EL HEROICA
BARRIO
MONIMBO

Children at Masaya

One hundred and sixteen men and women fell here in the fighting. The shacks and beat houses are scarred from the battle. "NO PASARAN" is scrawled next to the church. This Indian *barrio* was like slums in every Latin American or Caribbean town I've ever been in—on the outskirts of Lima, La Paz, Bolivia, Haiti's Port au Prince, Mexico City, Cuernavaca—dirt streets full of stray dogs, tin roof shacks, swinging-door *cantinas* smelling of piss and *pulque*, beer and mezcal (murderous at night, for people like Malcolm Lowry's Consul in *Under the Volcano*.)

The Revolution would change all that?

As soon as we arrive at a tiny plaza filled with an outdoor kitchen under a ridge-pole roof, three old musicians strike up a bright, whining tune—a fiddle and a *guitarrón*—and some barefoot Indian kids start dancing around in the dust. Ernesto is greeted warmly by the cook and his woman, like an old friend. We've obviously been expected. They seem to love him, they certainly respect him. A priest is a priest. Food has been set out, steaming, and now it is passed around. I eat and drink whatever is offered, though one of the journalists shakes his head. He's an old hand in Latin America, and knows what the guidebooks say: "Don't drink the water."

Ernesto makes a little speech, and we leave in our cars, for Granada, about an hour's drive. Granada has a plaza with colonial buildings and an ancient dusty elegance. Granada is Ernesto's birthplace, and his family house on the plaza was given to the Church by his grandmother. His large, well-off (if not rich) family is divided by the Revolution—some with it, some not. (*"No Pasaran"* is scrawled on

"Heroes and Martyrs" in Monimbó

At the waterfront, Lake Nicaragua, Granada

many walls.) We drive on through the town to the waterfront and end up at a waterfront pavilion for a fish lunch. Ernesto points out a well-dressed paunchy gentleman with his family who seems to be receiving various local businessmen who come up to him at the end of his long linen-covered table and almost bow as they shake hands, with a mixture of respect and fear, as if he still ran the town. The *patrón* receiving his homage. Some things never change, even in revolutions. Life goes on. Human nature goes on. The bourgeoisie will always be with us, no matter what the Marxists say. I think also of Roland Barthes' "the essential enemy (the bourgeois norm)" . . .

There is a little archipelago of islands in Lake Nicaragua just off Granada and to the southeast, and it is for them that we set out after lunch, in a long launch with canopy for shelter in the afternoon sun. About ten of us in the old wooden boat, with a gasoline engine groaning at the stern, and shortly we are passing through a Rousseau-like jungle, through small channels with overhanging vines between little islands. (Nicaraguan primitive painters, encouraged by Ernesto's Ministry of Culture, have portrayed their landscape in a manner similar to the Haitian primitives, and are being recognized as a school.)

Then we're out in the open again, passing over to another group of little jungle islets, some with small houses or shacks on them. A slight squall comes up, which reminds Fernando Silva of the local folk tale about a couple on their honeymoon who set out in a small boat on the lake. A big tempest comes up, and the boat is about to be swamped. The husband throws the underpants of the woman, stained with menstrual blood, on the waters. They immediately calm down . . .

We dock at one of the islands where there's a barbecue in progress, rather like a Hawaiian *luau*. We drink beer and sit around for awhile, hoping to buy some fried fish; but the boats didn't go out today—Sunday, and the wind is up . . . On the way back, we see the frame of a big excursion boat cast up on an island, its ribs rotting away. On the transom of the boat it says GENERAL SOMOZA. "When the boat sank, Somoza declined and sank!" someone shouts. There's general laughter.

It's late afternoon by the time we get back to Granada, and dark by the time we head up the slopes of the big volcano overlooking Managua, for the final stop. (The country has a series of volcanoes strung out the length of the land.) By the time we reach the edge of the huge crater it's pitch dark, and all we can see, peering over into the black, is thick smoke, with a burning smell as of sulphur. The huge mountain is like Mount Tamalpais in Marin County on a dark night, but here—someone shouts, laughing—is the smoldering "maw of revolution!" The poets lean over the railing in the smoke, gesticulating wildly at the hidden god below, uttering cries of mock defiance with bursts of wild laughter. A blast of smoke and heat sends them back. It is bigger than they are.

A wind has come up and it's shuddering cold. We huddle back to the cars and wend down the mountain, back into Managua. More *"No Pasaran"* graffiti on walls everywhere; but not a single *"Partido Comunisto."* I ask Luis Rocha how this

Somoza's boat

happens to be, while in Cuba even in 1960 there were Communist Party signs everywhere. He tells me that only about three percent of the population of Nicaragua are members of the CP, while about eight percent belong to another Socialist-oriented party, not pro-Soviet. (When I later tell this to a refugee from a mid-European Iron Curtain country, he points out to me that in all those countries dominated by Soviet Communism the actual membership in the CP is *always* very small.)

At the new sugarcane factory

January 30——Monday, and we're off early to see a new sugar cane plant in the process of construction, and an open prison farm. (We don't expect to be taken to the poorest of *barrios* of Managua, although we were free to go any time. Chris Felver visited one without escort one night and took a few photos in the fading light. When official visitors come to San Francisco, the tourist bureau doesn't take them to see the slums South of Market; they're shown the new symphony hall, the Opera House, the Golden Gate, or maybe Carol Doda performing native dances.)

"Timal" is being built near Tipitapa, not far out of Managua. We're driven there in a Mercedes inherited from the Somoza regime. (*Somocistas* owned the Mercedes dealership.) Huge pre-fab concrete hangars with high tin roofs. Other steel frame buildings going up. It's a model plan, and the assistant manager shows us the blueprints in his office and takes us around the works, carrying a walkie-talkie. The processing plant is set right in the center of the fields, and there will be a forest planted all around the cane fields to furnish the wood burned to run the plant. The whole project is to cost about $220 million U.S., and is supposed to be ready within two years, to produce 7,000 tons a day during the *zafra* (harvest) of 203 days. There is one other cane factory in Nicaragua: San Antonio, still privately owned. We walk through a huge warehouse where steel-hatted workers—looking like in any plant in

Workers (mostly Cuban) moving a Russian-built generator

the U.S.—are moving electrical equipment from East Germany and Russia. The generators have plates in English: "Made in USSR." There are quite a few Cuban workers. Some shake hands and pose for their pictures. No women working out here, but there are some in the construction offices . . .

We're off now to inspect "La Granja"—one of those "open farms" for prisoners, this one close to Managua. In a speech called "Eight Mistaken Theses" Tomás Borge recently refuted the accusation that Nicaragua violates human rights, insisting that his is a country "where there are no executions, where torture has been virtually eradicated, where prisoners, including *Somocistas*, have been located in work centers where they have a continuing relationship with their families, and many of them are under a regime of what we call 'open farms,' in which there are no sentries other than those of moral preachment and our own confidence in the prisoners: open farms without police and without bars . . . Witnesses of the treatment we grant prisoners are the International Red Cross, the Commission of Human Rights, a group of North American jurists headed by Mr. Ramsey Clark, writers of worldwide prestige such as Julio Cortázar, Carlos Fuentes, Gabriel Garcia Márquez, Günter Grass, and Graham Greene, among others."

Our guide for the visit is Captain Raúl Cordon, head of the regional prison system. It's working hours, and there's only a handful of prisoners hanging about the wooden barracks surrounded by wheat fields and cane. There's a central Rec room and some offices, the whole surrounded by a wire fence—nothing that couldn't be climbed. The

*Captain Raúl Cordon in
the trenches dug by prisoners*

captain tells us there were 8,000 prisoners in his region but now they're down to 2500. (Jesuit lawyers defended many *Somocistas* standing trial after the Sandinist victory, since most other lawyers claimed they couldn't be impartial.)

Somoza's chauffeur is head of the inmates, most of whom were in Somoza's National Guard and the EEBI Special Forces—"death squads," someone says. The chauffeur is exceedingly fat and full of smiles. He gives us a glowing account of life under the present setup. He has his own room and takes us there and passes around cigarettes. He picks up a guitar and strums a bit. The prison dentist, also a political prisoner, smiles at him . . . Outside, under dense rows of sugar cane, there are the deep trenches the prisoners dug when a USA-backed invasion was expected from the North. The cane would hide them. They asked for guns from the Sandinistas "to defend the country." They didn't get them.

We drink coffee out of tin cups with some of the inmates. It's strong enough to take your boots off. It's like ranch coffee outside of Douglas, Arizona. One of the coffee drinkers tells me he just got back from a week at home—they're allowed a week every six months, if they behave. And they have conjugal visits.

There's a "guest book" we're asked to sign, and we do, noting what Nobel Peace Prize winner Perez Esquivel wrote in the book: "With a fraternal greeting of peace & goodwill to all of the members of La Granja prison and their commitment to build a more just and humane society. Jan. 4 1984."

Back in the car as we head out, the captain shakes his head and smiles as

Father Cardenal with Somoza's chauffeur

Somoza's chauffeur stands by the gate, waving. *"Es un gran bandito,"* the captain says to us under his breath.

Back at the captain's HQ, we meet a more important political prisoner: Carlos Canales, former Minister of Health under Somoza. They tell me he was convicted for various monstrous medical swindles: 30 years. He's now under "house arrest." All his children, he tells us, are Sandinistas.

We're due to go to lunch with Tomás Borge, Minister of the Interior. Tortured for years in Somoza's prisons, after the Sandinist takeover he recognized one of his torturers in a prison lineup, and he is reported to have said, "My revenge is to have you shake my hand." Joan Baez made a song of this and sang it here in Spanish a couple of years ago.

He's a tough little number. He isn't in charge of internal security and intelligence for nothing. He's the only one of the three original founders of the Sandinista movement still alive. His face shows it, it's hard, it's been through it, you know it. He's a bull of a man, and he wears the uniform of a Commander of the Revolution. When we go with him to the public market for lunch, he drives his big van, with a couple of trucks full of soldiers before and after.

We've come to the big public *mercado* because Borge objected to plans for us to dine at one of the better restaurants. It's one of those typical new *mercados* under an overhanging roof, like the big one in Guadalajara—concrete stalls on a concrete floor, covering maybe two acres, an entire city block. Ernesto told me he ate here

Comandante Tomás Borge in his van

most every day; and Borge seems at home here. From the moment we get out of his van, the market vendors press around him, and there's a crush as we try to proceed to the long wooden tables in the middle of the market. I sit down on a bench with Borge as the people crowd around, and a television crew moves in with their camera. Borge orders *carne asada*, and he sets to the hunks of meat with both hands as several women vendors fill his ears full of complaints. They're mad about the government keeping food prices down so that they can't make out. Borge listens intently, nodding and eating, and looking into the women's faces. You can tell he likes contact with the people, acts like he's one of them; he is; he came up the hard way. He calls me *poèta* whenever he has a chance to speak to me, which isn't often. He says *poèta* with a mixture of respect and realism, as if he didn't expect much from me. (Before we part he gives me a fine edition of poetry by José Coronel Urtecho, *Paneles de Infierno*.)

At the moment we are still surrounded by a mass of people of all ages, old women in shawls, tough barefoot Indian mothers holding little kids, roundfaced and wide-eyed. A tiny little shoeshine boy sticks out his hand to shake mine. It is completely black with shoe polish. It's a joke, and everybody breaks up.

In a very few minutes Borge's through eating, and we push through the crowd, the TV following, as he inspects various stalls and produce, listening to the vendors' stories. One fishwife corners him and pours out her complaint. He takes her by both arms, almost embracing her, and looks in her face close up, listening intently. Finally we follow him up to the market manager's office on a mezzanine where he lays out the people's complaints to the man at the desk.

Tomás Borge (at right) entering the public market.

Tomás Borge (center) listening to the people

We make our way back out, and on the way he picks up a kid and dandles her (like any American politician) as the TV camera rolls. But he's got real affection for the kid who sucks her thumb bashfully. He puts her down and makes toward the van, on the way asking a pretty interpreter for her phone number. She refuses, politely. (One of his pamphlets is called *Women and the Nicaraguan Revolution*. It's a speech he gave in Léon in 1982 at a rally commemorating the fifth anniversary of the Nicaraguan women's movement, broadcast live. He presents a Marxist analysis of the history of women's oppression, explaining why only a socialist revolution, with the full participation of women, could eradicate such oppression.) Another book of his is: *Los Primeros Pasos: La Revolución Popular Sandinista*. The cover shows him holding a child.

Back in the driver's seat, he tells me, "These people really aren't *with* the Revolution. They're putting themselves first. The Revolution is for the consumer, not the merchant." When he drops me off in town, I look at the finely printed card in the book he gave me: his name without title, under a single silver star with red and black olive branches crossed beneath it.

It's time for the visit to *La Prensa*, the opposition newspaper, generally a pro-capitalist journal. Significantly, it's housed in the same two- or three-story building as the Bank of America. There aren't any guards at the entrance to the paper, as there are at the *San Francisco Chronicle* and *Examiner* these days. Simply a woman receptionist at the front desk, and we pass quickly up to the editorial offices and Pablo Antonio Cuadra, the very important poet and editor known for his opposition to the present regime, for both poetic and civil libertarian reasons. I knew a little about Cuadra, some of it from an interview with Rocio Fernández de Ulibarri of *La Nación* when Cuadra was passing through Costa Rica last fall on his way to an International PEN Club meeting in Venezuela. (First off I note that he was allowed to travel out of the country and was not in jail nor out of a job for that anti-Sandinist interview.) The introduction to it states in part:

> Cuadra's exile in his own country is a shipwreck on dry land. His vocation as a survivor is not easy, but his poetry and his freedom are as much a part of his Nicaragua as is the myth of Antaeus . . . There are few names in the literature of Nicaragua that mean as much as Pablo Antonio Cuadra . . . . An intellectual of his prestige within the opponents of the Sandinista regime is an indestructible enemy, because Cuadra is a synonym for Nicaragua—its lake, its land, its birds, its flowers, its roots, its fruit . . . To all this it is usual to add his work as a great exponent of literary activity in America, from *La Prensa Literaria* and the journal *El pez y la serpiente* . . . The person who has been the most influential in the literature and general culture of his nation is today the interpreter of an internal exile. One excludes the poet and puts him aside like all those who maintain an independ-

Pablo Antonio Cuadra at **La Prensa**

ent point of view or defend the freedom of the individual, above all that of the writer towards the power of the state. Despite his international prestige, he has been called "a seller-out of his country."

In the interview itself he said:

> They are killing me but I'm not leaving. I am too old to seek adventures. Unless they take me with a crane and put me on the border, I'm not leaving Nicaragua.
>
> I am against the direction of the revolution taken by the Sandinistas. If I have stayed within the country and kept my position in *La Prensa* and the literary journal *El pez y la serpiente* it is exactly because I believe that the attitude of directing culture, censorship and the creation of a conscience in the service of an ideology . . . is fateful for a culture. That is why I am in a rather disagreeable struggle. And my obligation as a poet is to maintain the flag of resistance against the tremendous harm being done to the culture of Nicaragua.
>
> If the author is politically a Communist, Social Democrat, or Christian Democrat, that is a personal compromise which will be reflected in some manner in his work, because there cannot be a division between a man and his creation, but if this is imposed in favor of a thesis, what he does is didacticism and kills his work.

The poet then spoke of the experience of Pablo Neruda and Ernesto Cardenal, as poets in the service of an ideology, stating that their great failures coincided with the moment they started producing didactic or proselytizing literature.

The poet went on to ask:

> From what does culture spring? From lack of conformity. And what is the instrument of lack of conformity? *Criticism*. It is the only means which makes possible man's perfection. If criticism is suspended and we are obliged to conform, we become like the chimpanzee. This is what happens to a culture which lacks a critical sense. I have often repeated the sentence: every revolution becomes stagnant without criticism.
>
> Facing the instrumentation of that direction, the writer is the only valid critic. He is his own critic, but if someone on high tells him "this work lacks a class consciousness, a popular sense, and accessible language," then the writer loses his originality and creative power and becomes a clerk . . . Class consciousness, applied to a work, also kills it. The writer should have the consciousness of Sancho and also that of Quixote, that of king and that of vassal, that of exploiter and that of the exploited . . .
>
> They always say that creative freedom is a requirement of the revolution. Nevertheless, a short time ago they published the famous speech of Fidel Castro to the intellectuals, a speech which cost a

multitude of exiles. Then, why if we are in agreement that creative freedom is a requirement of the revolution, does one wish to put literature at its service or impose the arts as weapons of the revolution? As soon as literature begins to be in the service of something it stops being literature and turns to propaganda.

Cuadra concluded the interview by stating that at *La Prensa* threats extend beyond the paper shortage—"Their rigid censorship enters as a control over freedom of expression." But *La Prensa* represents "precisely the part of the revolution which has gone astray, *the libertarian part of the battle.* We are fighting for a justice with freedom and for a freedom with justice. Both are inseparable. That is why *La Prensa* is a bastion of the complement of an incomplete revolution. If it were closed it would be cutting Nicaragua's tongue out."

The first thing Cuadra said when I walked into his office (Ernesto, significantly, did not accompany me on the visit) was that he was very sorry *La Prensa* could not publish my poetry because the Sandinist government would not give them paper to publish their literary supplement. I agreed that that was certainly bad, but the Sandinist justification for this seemed valid. There were priorities. It took U.S. dollars to buy newsprint, and it took U.S. dollars to buy medical supplies, technical equipment, and consumer goods which were in desperately short supply. (Chris Felver couldn't find AA batteries for his camera nor any black-and-white film in stores in Managua. There was fresh produce and meat in the markets, but most manufactured goods were expensive and scarce.) These things, in the eyes of the Sandinist government, had priority over newsprint for literature.

I also felt it fair to remind him that *La Prensa* itself was not so long ago about to shut down because they couldn't get newsprint, and that the government furnished them dollars to buy it and continue publishing. I also felt it fair to ask him if total freedom of the press didn't also require *responsibility* on the part of the press for what it printed? In a democratic society—where the news is "tailored" by private owners of the press rather than by direct government censorship—there is pressure within the press itself to maintain standards of "evidence, proof and disclosure." Unless the editors are totally cynical, don't they have to believe that what they print is the truth? In which case, what of the report on Fidel Castro by one Carlos Montaner (a Cuban editor who left their revolution and lives out of the country) published in *La Prensa?* In the article Montaner stated that Fidel Castro is fat, old, sick, and about to die. Could the editors of *La Prensa* really believe that is the truth? To which Pablo Antonio Cuadra shrugged and said with a smile, "That's the sixty-four dollar question."

As a civil libertarian I would have to add, however, that even if *La Prensa* published *nothing but lies*, it should still be allowed to publish them. An answer to this came later from Ernesto Cardenal. It was a subject that often came up. In one conversation, he said: "Try and get an article advocating the overthrow of the United States government into any major newspaper in the U.S.—or even try getting a Marxist article in *The New York Times*." And he pointed out that Nicaragua was in a state of war, the Reagan administration and the CIA having admitted they were trying to overthrow the Sandinist government by undercover military means. And in a state of war, even the greatest democracies resort to strict censorship of the press in military and economic matters—witness the British in the Malvina Islands, the Israelis in occupied areas of Lebanon, and most recently the USA in Grenada. In these areas, censorship restricted foreign journalists especially—which evidently has never been the case in Nicaragua. (Bill Finnegan, the correspondent for *New Age*, told me later he had not heard of any censorship in the transmittal of news by U.S. journalists inside Nicaragua.)

Ernesto Cardenal sent me an official statement of his own on the issue, when I had returned to the U.S., and this is a translation of it:

MINISTRY OF CULTURE, NICARAGUA
Government of National Reconstruction

6 April 1984

With respect to censorship, I don't believe there is any important writing by any of our leaders defending it. In fact, we don't like it and don't want it, and have it only because we're in a state of war. In any state of war there has to be recourse to these means. A state of emergency is declared, a law that permits any steps that might be needed for defense. We're engaged in a war, an undeclared and "undercover" war but a war that everyone is aware of; even the United States Congress publicly approves financing it. And the newspaper *La Prensa* openly defends the enemy, defends the C.I.A.'s actions, and employs all the Reagan administration's arguments. In the United States, there's a lot of publicity about an opposition newspaper being censored in Nicaragua, something we're obliged to do because of the war, but there's no concern expressed about other Latin American countries where opposition newspapers are not censored because there simply are no opposition newspapers (Guatemala, El Salvador, Chile, Uruguay, Paraguay). In any case, this censorship will end in May when the electoral campaign begins. Then they won't attack Nicaragua for this reason, but will look for many other reasons to attack us.

translated by Barbara Paschke

Statements on censorship by other members of the government include this one by Daniel Ortega Saavedra, the coordinator of the ruling junta, in a speech reprinted in a Ministry of Culture publication, *Hacia una Politica Cultural*:

If there is any advice we have for artists, it is that they develop their imagination, their creative capacities as they themselves see fit. What is needed is to bring up everything that was accumulated and repressed, to develop that, without ignoring what there is outside which will help us develop and move ahead, free of any restrictions, without feeling pressed to give our work a certain tilt in order to stay on good terms with the Revolution, to the extent that we are capable of being ever more creative, of generating new forms, new ideas, of continually exercising our imaginations, and breaking with all subservient forms of thinking. Our thinking cannot be shaped by predetermined formulas, it must be completely open . . .

I parted from Sr. Cuadra amiably enough. (Ernesto had said he was the only major poet against the Sandinist regime.) I believe we understood each other, as poets. He wanted to talk poetry, not politics. We exchanged books of poetry. The inscription in his book read: *"Su lector y amigo*—Pablo Antonio Cuadra."

Quite aware of the "totalitarian intolerance" often exercised by the Left as well as the Right in the U.S., I shook his hand and wished him well as we parted. If the Sandinistas really believed, as they insisted, on a "democratic pluralism" in their government, I wished to be a part of it.

At about nightfall we go to meet Jaime Wheelock, the Minister of Agriculture, and sit down with him in a big museum-like room at his headquarters. There are plants everywhere and big, framed Indian paintings and tapestries.

He tells me he would rather talk to poets than politicians, and I believe him. He seems a very literate man—a young intellectual one might meet at Columbia University. He tells me that before the Revolution the farmworkers lived like sharecroppers in *The Grapes of Wrath* and that now for the first time they are being organized in collectives or cooperatives, at a somewhat better living wage. They are at least getting control of their own means of livelihood. Field workers are at present getting about $3.50 (U.S.) a day, but under the cooperatives they will earn more by the year, participating in the income. (Wheelock is a lawyer and is credited with being one of the main theoreticians of the Revolution.)

He tells me he's more interested in what poets have to say than what he might hear from government functionaries. He says poets are honored in his country and that he would like to offer me a house on one of the little islands off Granada where we went on Sunday, if I would come and work for them in the cultural field.

He has a very calm, straightforward look. He's handsome in his uniform, and he poses for a photo in the courtyard when we are leaving. It is dark, and Chris Felver is adjusting his flash as Wheelock stands there against the shrubbery, looking quite serious. After the picture is taken, Wheelock says, "That's how Somoza's guards killed some people—'shooting' them with cameras."

Comandante Jaime Wheelock

He walks us to our car, and we part. I had felt such rapport with the man that I had neglected to ask him the most pertinent question, from the point of view of American labor. Why had the government suspended the workers' right to strike? Or perhaps I hadn't asked because I knew what the answer would be, and he knew I knew, so why go through the charade? At the present stage of socialist regimes in the world, the answer is always the same: expediency. In the present desperate state of the economy in Nicaragua, strikes are disastrous to the fragile industry in question. As with censorship, the difference between capitalism and socialism is that the control is exercised by the state in the latter and by the "private sector" in the former. But even in the U.S., the government had more than once enacted strike-breaking legislation.

(Looking back, I recollect Wheelock did point out that President Reagan's action in cutting out the Nicaraguan sugar quota to the U.S. had tended to cut down on the private sector, something which Reagan in fact wanted everywhere to augment. When the sugar quota was withdrawn, the privately-owned San Antonio plant was faced with financial disaster; it was only by finding buyers among non-aligned countries that bankruptcy was averted.)

January 31——We had not yet visited the Ministry of Culture itself, and today we go to visit Cardenal in his office in a villa which had belonged to Somoza. It is a beautiful little house set in a park in a grove. There are only about five big rooms but there had been over a dozen bathrooms. There were bathrooms off of bathrooms. Ernesto's office was a bathroom. No more than 10 by 15 feet, it is now cluttered with heaps of books and art work. Among the books I find the book of photographs by the American photographer killed on the frontier, *Nicaragua: the War of Liberation*. Printed in Germany, it includes poems by Cardenal, Cross's good friend. Among the many other books published by the Ministry of Culture, I find Fernando Silva's *Poesía*; Bosco Centeno's *Puyonearon los granos*; Daisy Zamora's *La Violenta Espuma*; *Talleres de Poesía* by students in poetry workshops all over the country; *Poesía campesina de Solentiname* by farmworkers on the island of Solentiname; José *Coronel Urtecho's Paneles de Infierno*; *Hacia una política cultural: de la revolución popular Sandinista* with an introduction by Daisy Zamora; and various issues of the beautiful literary revue, *Nicaráuac*. There are also a dozen issues of the Ministry's poetry review, *Poesia Libre*, and I note that one issue opens with translations of Ezra Pound by Urtecho and Cardenal. Attesting to their "pluralism" in culture at least, I also see copies of the dissident Cuadra's literary review, *el Pez y la*

Serpiente, a most important cultural journal. (Its literary advisors include Octavio Paz in Mexico, Mario Vargas Llosa in Peru, Ernesto Sábato in Argentina, Luis Rosales in Spain, Ledo Ivo in Brazil.)

As we're leaving it occurs to me someone should write a satirical porno novel: *Los Baños de Somoza*.

In the late afternoon we get to another publishing house, Editorial Nueva Nicaragua, where there is a small reception in progress, and we meet the director, Roberto Diaz, as well as Sergio Ramirez, an important novelist, editor, and *comandante* in the National Directorate.

We stand around the punch bowl, meeting various authors whose names I don't quite catch, as is usually the case at similar affairs in the States. I note on the walls the covers of recent books from this press: Julio Cortázar's *Nicaragua tan violentamente dulce*; Luis Rocha's *Phocas*; Tomás Borge's *Carlos, el amanecer ya no es una tentación*.

Unfortunately I did not have a chance to get into any substantive conversation with Sergio Ramirez, but I knew that the American Margaret Randall had interviewed him recently, and I knew he was a leader of the literary movement "Ventana" which had arisen in 1960 as a literary or cultural expression of the political movement toward liberation. In view of what Pablo Antonio Cuadra had said against the Revolution, it is interesting to read Ramirez' pro-Revolutionary sentiments pub-

(L to R): LF; Comandante Sergio Ramirez; Father Cardenal

lished in Margaret Randall's interview (in the Canadian journal *Impulse*, Summer, 1984):

The Revolution has provided culture to an extent without precedent in Nicaragua's history. And we notice that effect in the cultural area because it is a sensitive field in which we have a priority interest. The revolution has provided schools, many classrooms, children's vaccinations, rural public health posts, stores, and enormous multiplication of resources, even with regard to scarcity and poverty. There is a centrifugal force, which is people's power in action.

And this people's power is what makes our culture different from all other Central American cultures. I feel that we are in a stage of cultural ebullition, continuously boiling at high temperatures. What are the results going to be? We don't know yet because the mass is still incandescent, shapeless.

I can't tell you that there is a narrative of the Revolution, a novel or a poetry of the Revolution, but that is being cooked here, at a high temperature. And I believe the results are going to be extraordinary, the results are going to be great poets, story-writers, theatre people, painters, sculptors, photographers, musicians, and dancers, because that's the Revolution's strength: moving the enormous human mass in tasks which it had never known itself capable of before. The result will be outstanding, creative individuals.

We are going to have a new culture, the foundations of which have been laid in the proper manner, with enough creative freedom, without dogmatism, without sectarianism, and strengthening freedom, the very dynamics of the Revolution. That seems very important to me: the fact that no one here has ever written, on how to sculpt or paint, but that rather the only thing we did was to create the possibilities to create.

The most important thing in Nicaragua is that there is absolute freedom for creativity as well as for the participation in creativity. It is something in which anyone can take part. Here we don't have a cultural elite made up of all the people who now have that possibility. And while we keep that creative freedom, the possibility of participation, the results are going to be good.

But it is time to leave for a meeting with the Association of Sandinista Cultural Workers (ASTC). When we arrive at their arts center there are about fifty men and women already assembled outdoors, seated in a large circle. It was billed as a "colloqui," but it seemed I was to make a speech. Suddenly I wish I had in my pocket a list of the "best minds of my generation" and of the greatest and most respected establishment writers in the USA who are publicly and actively supporting the Sandinista regime—but such a list is short. (How many of our most famous novelists, for instance, have bothered to take the two-and-a-half-hour flight from Miami and see for themselves what's going on here? Unfortunately, we don't have many

At the meeting of the Association of Sandinista Cultural Workers

with the international consciousness of a Carlos Fuentes, the Mexican novelist recently at Harvard. Our literary activists seem to be confined—with a few valiant exceptions—to the younger, lesser known, dissident writers, while most of the great ones in their positions at the top of the establishment continue to maintain a loud silence.)

As these sanguine and lugubrious thoughts fill my head, the artists and intellectuals of Nicaragua sit awaiting my words. All right, then. From the activist poets and the politically dormant poets of my country, I bring you greetings and wishes for your survival against all odds. Not being an ambassador of that imperial plutocratic government in Washington, I can only give you my somewhat eccentric dissident view of what's going on . . . And I launched into a diatribe on nationalism in general, which is definitely not what they wanted to hear.

(A young nation just struggling free of centuries of colonialism, Sandinist Nicaragua sees nationalism as the way to independence. Carlos Fuentes said, "Mexico found that it had to be a nation before it could be a democracy." And, if this is true, Soviet Communism is not what the Nicaraguan people really want as their vehicle of change. A former director of national planning in Nicaragua, Father Xavier Gorastiaga, said, "There arc a lot of Marxist tendencies in Central America, but they are not what I would call dogmatic European Marxist tendencies. What exists is a sort of *Creole Marxism*, a convergence of nationalism, Christianity, and Marxism." It would seem, then, in this *crisis of decolonization*, what is most needed is some form of government which will allow the mass of the people here to realize their own special identity and their own civil and economic freedom. And what is the identity of the people of Nicaragua? Is it not related—in language and ethnicity—to that of *all* the Central American countries? And they have reason to make common cause with each other, to defend themselves against piecemeal attacks and attrition from abroad. Is not Alaska safer from annexation by Russia or some other Asian power now, as one of the United States? And thus it would seem to the best interest of the USA to promote just what the USA seems to resist—the full development of the Contadora movement, leading—if carried to its logical conclusion—to the creation of a *United States of Central America*, in which each little country here would give up part of its "states rights"—just as the United States found it necessary at the end of its Civil War, just as "states rights" on the international level (national sovereignty, the absolute veto, etc.) must to some degree be given up by all nations of the world if they are not to destroy each other finally. Another way of putting it—the one hope is to make the whole earth *literally* one "global village," beyond civil war. But perhaps Central America must be one nation before it can be a democracy—a new nation (conceived in liberty, etc.) whose states will be safe from being picked off one by one by foreign powers or ideologies—in effect preventing that very "domino" action which U.S. foreign policy has used to justify its overt covert war on Communism in Central America.)

Meanwhile, back at the cultural meeting, the floor was open to questions, and what they especially wanted to hear about was writing and especially poetry in the USA today. I gave them my view that North American poetry right now seems to be in a deep sleep or, hopefully, in a state of gestation. Some writers are just too well fed, by government grants or university writing programs. Some are not so well fed but lack the stimulus provided by war, rapid change in society, or revolution as in Nicaragua now. Poets are not especially honored in our land, having for the most part abdicated any vatic or prophetic role—with some large exceptions. As such, poetry has been relegated to a most ephemeral place—positioned as "filler" in most large publications, though published profusely by small presses throughout the land. *What it takes is inspiration, and hunger.* Thus it is the poets of various minorities, still with their own revolutions to win, who seem to have the most to say (with the most force) in North America now (as witness for instance the Latino writers of San Francisco's Mission district and New York's *Newyoricanos*.)

As an afterthought, it occurs to me now, that a true civil libertarian would have asked these Sandinista Cultural Workers whether any of them would be allowed to be in their Union if they openly declared themselves to be gadflies or "enemies of the State."

I was introduced at the meeting by Rosario Murillo, the Director of the Association, and she too was interviewed for the Canadian magazine, *Impulse*, about this time. In this interview she said in part:

Often it is said that the Nicaraguan Revolution is a revolution of poets, and this can be witnessed in the daily lives of the people . . . We say this is a country of artists, of men and women proud of their culture. For this reason, the Sandinista government insists on the development of cultural activities as a part of the development of the revolutionary process. A majority of artists took part in the struggle for liberation. At the barricades, we danced, and invented home-made weapons, based on the age-old techniques of our artisan-artists. To hide their faces, our people used masks from traditional folkloric dances. There was always an interaction between art, culture, and revolutionary struggle. This is why the triumph of the Revolution signifies the triumph of culture . . . On the day of the victory, the Ministry of Culture was created; the same day a campaign was created which would become the Literacy Campaign, eradicating 80% of the illiteracy in this country . . . We have poetry workshops in the armed forces, state security police, air force, and, of course, in factories, barrios, and the countryside . . . Our slogan is that art is a Sandinista trench, that art is a weapon for the people in defense of the revolutionary process . . . Artists have been highly valued by the Sandinista Revolution, and their specificities have been considered, as the case of the Patriotic Military Service Law (the draft) where it has been decided that artists who have to join the army are joining as artists . . . Our fundamental work in the case of escalated aggression is to fight with our song, poetry, etc., as long as we can . . . This work is very important in creating consciousness of the injustice of U.S. foreign policy regarding Central America. . . . There is need to respect the rights of self-determination, independence and, above all, the right to live as human beings. This is the right which was our conquest with the Revolution. This is the right they won't take away from us. For this right, our whole people is willing to fight, but we have confidence that the American people, a sensitive and honest people, will respond positively when they have the right information.

It was not my poetry reading that night in the open-air theatre of the Plaza Pedro Joaquin Chomorro, nor Ernesto Cardenal's translations of it, which was significant. It was the circumstances and events around it which were more to the point of this book. (And this observation itself illustrates how poetry is constantly pushed to the back burner. Not that my poem on the Cowboy in the White House saddle, swinging his lasso over Central America, wasn't "relevant" enough.)

When I came off stage at the end of the reading, there was a stringer crew from CBS waiting to interview me.

Q: What are your impressions of Nicaragua?

LF: It's a humane revolution—at least it would seem so on the surface. I realize I'm on a guided tour—the Sandinista leaders seem to be using what Carlos Fonseca called temperance and fortitude.

Q. Isn't that the kind of revolution which would especially upset the Reagan administration?

LF: Yes, indeed, for it is especially hard to justify subverting such a human revolution—if such it is. And a revolution that liberates people from their traditional economic slavery isn't exactly what corporate people in the USA want to hear. It's the have and have-nots and Central America has been a cheap labor market for the U.S. for centuries. That's the real "domino" effect the U.S. is afraid of. The idea of "freedom" knows no boundaries. The trouble is the U.S. press doesn't always play fair, as you have. They blow up the slightest incident to show it is not humane, that it is a totalitarian dictatorship, that there is torture, that it's a police state—none of which I have found to be true—and it's a self-fulfilling prophecy. The reality becomes what you say the reality is. Mr. Reagan is doing the same thing—

Q: Thank you for your kind remarks!

The interview was never aired. I wasn't the kind of hot news they wanted. During the reading I had noted that it was not exactly a turn-away crowd—the amphitheater was about half empty, or half full, at the most. (I am no Yevtuchenko nor was meant to be!) The Revolution wanted to bring poetry to the masses; but the masses did not come to the poetry. The audience turned out to be mostly students, poets, and wandering U.S. militants of various sorts—including a Pacifica Foundation interviewer. Thus fares poetry on the barricades . . .

Presenting the seed from Pasternak's grave

Fernando Silva, the poet and doctor whom I met on our Sunday excursion, was another with whom I felt an immediate humane rapport (and it was in fact he who stimulated it by exclaiming within an hour of our meeting, "We're brothers!") He gave me a flower after a while, saying *La Bruja* grew where nothing else would, in the most unexpected places. (There was another flower pointed out to me known as *La Dormilona* or *Dormirada* which was always asleep. When you touch it, it folds up. Definitely not a flower of revolution.) I wrote the following poem out of a certain "revolutionary euphoria" and presented it at the reading—one can put it down as naive agitprop—but perhaps it is a naiveté worth saving. And it related well to the seed I brought from Pasternak's grave.

LA BRUJA: FLOWER OF REVOLUTION

In the fields of hunger
in the lakes of thirst
under the hills of hunger
under the volcanoes
Wherever there is nothing
wherever there is no sign of green
like birds on the edge of a volcano
like arctic flowers that never fade
in the still white nights
in the nights of black coral
in the dark nights of everybody's soul
these *bruja* flowers
like fireflies seeking light

in the forests in the jungles on the beaches
on frontiers and mountains
in the Sierra Maestra on our imagination
in houses in streets in alleyways
in offices of the rich
in restaurants of the fat and bored
in campesino cantinas
in workshops of the mind
in churches full of dead popes
And in the shacks in the dirt streets of Monimbó
sprouts this foolhardy flower
this magic purple flower
this brave *flor bruja*
sprouts straight up
in the light of a new day
And it will even sprout up
out of the barrels of rifles
out of the barrels of cannons
when at last all guns are laid down
and buried in gardens
this so brave so foolish *flor bruja*
flor curandera
flower of revolution

Managua 30 Enero 1984

*In a barrio, Managua—
flowers of revolution*

February 1——We were scheduled to go to the northern frontier on the Honduran border. But, whether out of concern for the safety of Ernesto or myself, our trip has been diverted to the southern Costa Rican front where the war is at the moment less dangerous.

We head south in a little convoy, a Land Rover with three soldiers ahead of us, Ernesto, Chris Felver, and myself next in the Toyota sedan, then another sedan with Ken Silverman and Bill Finnegan, followed by another jeep with soldiers. They're communicating with checkpoints by walkie-talkie as we proceed into open country, rather like coastal farmland in California or Chile. South of Masaya, the vegetation begins to be more verdant and tropical; palms and bananas, fields of cane, coffee, and cotton, bone-colored Brahman cattle with horns, houses and shacks and barns with tin roofs, mango and yucca . . . flocks of egrets nested in trees like great white flowers.

It's about a two-hour drive to Cibalsa in the Rivas area. We wheel in there, preceded by walkie-talkie identification, get out to stretch and meet the local captain. In his office in a barracks Bill Finnegan notes the following books on a shelf:

Manual of Marxism and Leninism
Complete Works of Lenin

The captain of the guard at Cibalsa

Comedies and Histories of Shakespeare
Jaime Wheelock's *Nicaragua: Imperialism and Dictatorship* (four copies)
Fernandos Rojas, *La Celestina*
Dostoevsky, *Crime and Punishment*
(All in Spanish)

Here was once a big center for Somoza's National Guard, his most important forces in the South. Ernesto tells me some 2000 Sandinistas were engaged in the heavy fighting, with 200 casualties a day. It's open country with little cover, with low mountains to the West and South, and Lake Nicaragua to the East. Two huge volcanoes joined by an isthmus in the lake—Ometépé.

This is near where a trans-Pacific canal was once proposed—in a deal the Chamorro family was involved in—with Lake Nicaragua used as the central part of the plan. If it had gone through, the history of Nicaragua would have been changed radically, with the country perhaps in the same economic and political position as Panama today—a fast change from banana republic to military bivouac.

Ernesto tells me the Rivas area was the old Indian center in pre-Hispanic times. The *cacique* (Indian chief) met the Spaniards at Cibalsa, and he asked them:

Why is there day and night?
Is the earth round or flat?
Why do you want so much gold?

Command post in Rivas area

Bulletin board at Sopa

The Spanish called the lake *La Mar Dulce,* said it was sweet to their taste, and that it should be theirs.

We take off south again, after numerous radio checks, and reach Sopa, three kilometers or so from the Costa Rican border. The last heavy fighting around here was at Cardenas on September 28th. On the outdoor board at the HQ here there are bulletins and clippings posted with national, international, sports, and cultural news. There is a paste-up of a poem by Leonel Rugama who died fighting in Managua in 1970. The poem is *Las casas quederon llenas de humo* ("The Houses were Filled with Smoke." It happens to be in the City Lights anthology, *Volcán.*)

This is our first look at the People's Militia. Young boys in green fatigues—most look 15 or 16 years old. One is 12, another 13. (They'd be in school, Ernesto says, if it weren't for Reagan's policies.) The Army is small but the Militia is big, mostly volunteer, he tells me. A recent draft prompted by expectations of an immediate invasion was not very successful, some families spiriting their children away to other countries (according to one newspaper report). Here the recruits look mostly like local country boys, part Indian, many from Ometépé.

After 15 minutes, we head south again, through a big truck checkpoint, directly to Peñas Blancas at the border. It takes just five minutes, and we roll up to the destroyed buildings of the immigration and customs offices—hit by mortars from the Costa Rican side. Ernesto tells us 200 anti-Sandinistas got this far and were stopped by 28 Sandinistas. Since they couldn't go any further, they burned and destroyed everything before retiring. There is a bullet hole in the one water tank, which leaks steadily.

The People's Militia at Peñas Blancas

In the ruins

We walk around in the ruins of one building, strewn with rubble, broken glass, plaster, and shattered furniture. Ernesto finds a burned, melted plastic doll and holds it up.

About 25 of the Militia line up in formation for review by our party and especially for Ernesto. A visit from the Minister of Culture is an event, and he hasn't been down here in months. He addresses them, softly, like a priest. Then one very young soldier in ranks cries out a challenge (a *consigna*), and the whole troop sings out a password in response. Sandinista slogans. This is repeated by different men in the ranks, with the rest singing out their valiant answers. The Indian faces, the expressions in the dark faces of these very young soldiers when they cry out their slogans (*"Patria o morir"*) is a mixture of defiance, pride, and *terror* . . .

In a few minutes we are back in the cars again, heading for a jungle camp—a farm deep in the woods on the border, the militia quartered in a big shed with thatched roof. Grenade launchers, AK47's, automatic weapons with Russian markings, lined up on racks. There's also another of those bulletin boards with current news tacked up. We walk around inspecting everything. The soldiers sing out a few *consignas* as we leave them in the dust. It's their life, their future. (Are they at the heart of the real, or are we?)

Edén Pastora's forces just over the hills don't call themselves "contras" because they are not against the original Revolution. They feel the Sandinistas have betrayed the ideals of Sandino by becoming a totalitarian state backed by Cuba and the

The defenses at Peñas Blancas

USSR. One adherent of Pastora, a Nicaraguan exile who came to see me in San Francisco, told me—it seemed with a touch of disbelief in his own words—that things were worse now in Nicaragua than they had been under Somoza!

This is quite absurd, even by anti-Sandinista standards, if any of the real history of Somoza is known. Here is a short rundown of that history and the Revolution, taken from an account by Felix Masud, in *Red Bass* (Tallahassee, Fla., Winter, 1983); it comes from an obviously leftist publication, but most of the facts cannot be disputed:

> Anastasio Somoza Garcia, the first of three Somozas to rule the country, came to power in 1936 as head of the newly created, United States-trained national guard. With a powerful military machine, the Somoza family ruled Nicaragua like a medieval fief. The best lands were divided among the key generals and the family, who came to own more than 20% of the richest lands in the country. Other Somoza assets included the national airline, banks, import-export firms, sugar, cotton, and tobacco interests, cattle, real estate property abroad (much of it in South Florida) and millions of dollars in Swiss bank accounts (estimated at $1 billion).
>
> For 43 years the Somoza dynasty enjoyed the full political, economic, and military support from the United States. And for 43 years, no one in Washington ever asked the Somozas to protect democratic freedoms, hold elections, or free the economy from the dynasty's stranglehold. In

fact, with little regard to the human rights situation in Nicaragua, President Franklin Delano Roosevelt once referred to Somoza as being an "S.O.B., but *our* S.O.B.".

After almost twenty years of armed struggle and over 50,000 dead, the dictatorship was finally overthrown on July 19, 1979. The dictator, however, had left his odious mark. The country was in ruins after months of wanton bombings during the final stages of the insurrection. The treasury had been sacked and left empty by Somoza and his henchmen. Illiteracy was over 50%, unemployment over 40%, malnutrition ran rampant, and the national debt ran in the billions. Under these conditions the Sandinistas began their gigantic, but hopeful task of national reconstruction.

Today, after four years of revolution, despite a lack of material resources and a war mobilization, the Sandinistas are making good on their promises. No one can deny that the life of most Nicaraguans has been improved dramatically. Illiteracy has been reduced 12%, and more than a million Nicaraguans are in schools (40% of the population). Free medical care is available in even the most remote corners of the country. The infant mortality rate has dropped from 120 per 1000 to 90 per 1000. A far reaching agrarian reform provides land for anyone who wants it and will work. Unemployment has dropped significantly, and food production is at an all-time high.

Sandinistas in the jungle camp on the Costa Rican border

In a port, on the way back to Managua someone said: "The Nicaraguan Navy!"

It was a long drive back to Managua, and the dusk was falling by the time we came down to the city, passing a big McDonald's with long lines waiting to be served. (Did I dream it had colonial architecture? On one wall was spray-painted "*NO PASARAN!*")

It was a free night for us, and we had supper at the house. On local television there was the Simon & Garfunkle show from Central Park (N.Y.), Emile Zola's "Teresa," and the Bolshoi Ballet.

The houseboy or waiter at our house, by the way, said it might be dangerous for us to go out by ourselves at night. (We might be taken for Ugly Americans?) The "houseboy" was a soldier on leave from the front. I thought of Ernesto's "no servants and no masters."

I believe it was that night about 1 a.m. that Chris Felver went out with our guide Nadia to a disco, and here is his description: "Typical joint with music so loud that there was difficulty talking. As Nadia went to the powder room I leaned on a gigantically large loudspeaker watching the dancers and thinking everywhere is like everywhere else this time of night. Tired of sound and motion, I wandered over to the 'obvious American' Nadia had pointed out to me as we entered. Sure enough, he was a Marine attached to the U.S. Embassy who had tried being a journalist in Baltimore before enlisting two years ago. 'Nicaragua is where I've taken all my leave the last two years,' this powerful black man says, looking me straight in the eyes. 'There is no better place for me, I really don't want to leave, there is just no color barrier,' he tells me candidly. 'But all the Nicaraguans have to do is take any of the Russian MIG's and the U.S. will invade tomorrow,' he assures me, as if he had inside information.

"Since we're still looking for a drink, we head to another outdoor cafe that is all but closing up, and at this moment a group of men pass by, offering me a cigarette, and I realize they are all gay. I take the cigarette and make some funny comment they all pick up on, but Nadia brushes them aside and bids them '*Buenas noches.*' She laughs: 'They tolerate that kind here, but don't promote them.'"

Chris Felver's notes on his *first* night in Nicaragua went like this: "Luz Marina and our interpreter Nadia take me to a local restaurant for a touch of local night life. Next to the steak restaurant is the bar, typical, with piano player and stand-up bass. During the first song a man falls over a table and reveals a big revolver stuck in his pants. His friends help him to his feet, and another round of drinks comes. Everyone is dressed in polo shirts and casual dress, with a remarkable starched dress with large puffed sleeves on one young woman. We pick up with this group and head through town on a wild half-crazed drive to a residential section. Later I find out that I am drinking Stoly vodka with *Comandante guerrillero* Richard Lugo Kantz, a hero in the Sandinista victory. Before entering his house, we relieve ourselves in the side yard and discuss the stars centering on Orion. His house has an elaborate audiovisual system, two cassette recorders, a Betamax ½″ video system, and a full bar of liquors international. On the porch are two bulldogs and a chow, with the largest bulldog in a hammock peering questioningly at me. We play the Beatles and suddenly it is the late

Sixties again with the Revolver album on the stereo. My first night in Nicaragua and I am asked the whole political gambit. Cornered, I propose a toast to the Revolution and life in this room in general. All the while there is a gentleman in the house who is removed from the conversation and I realize he is the bodyguard. We finally leave after the *Comandante* has asked me to go fishing early in the morning but I decline as we must meet Ernesto at 8:30 sharp. This is not the evening I had planned when asking to go out on the town, as my Spanish has not come back yet and translating is still difficult, yet the next day the American journalists tell me that ordinarily living here I would never have gotten to spend a night trysting with that particular group."

Chris' notes on another night also have their place here: "Later at our house, we meet a beautiful young *compañera* and her mother, and after a while she leaves her mother and I follow her out to the pool. While dipping our feet in the water, she tells me 'revolution is life' and there is no existence without it. Later, in a hammock, I ask, 'Where is love in your life?' She tells me of her lover in South America who is also fighting for freedom with all his heart and soul. 'Love is the revolution and that is life.' She wouldn't go for any man who wasn't committed as she was . . . "

Chris Felver, the photographer,
in front of Russian-built copter

February 2——To Solentiname today by helicopter. I had especially asked to visit Ernesto's island, way to the South at the far end of Lake Nicaragua. It was there that Ernesto had founded a contemplative community during the Somoza days. The National Guard had razed the place, destroying everything but the little chapel, and Ernesto had had to flee abroad. Now it had been mostly restored, and Ernesto had been back, but not recently. He'd been wanting to go for months, in fact hoped to retire there but felt he couldn't while there was work to do for the Revolution.

So into the big Russian-made military copter at eight—it was too far to go in one day by boat, and we were leaving the country the next day. A woman who had seven children in the fighting (one killed) was among the passengers. And there were Ernesto, our guide Nadia, Silverman and Finnegan, and two soldiers, plus the pilot and two crew. Writing in my notebook, I was surprised to see we were already in the air—not the slightest feeling of motion. Suddenly we were 1000 feet up and scudding over the brown land. Ernesto is reading the daily, *El Nuevo Diario*, with a story about Martinez Rivas winning the annual Rubén Darío poetry prize. (He's one of the three big poets of Ernesto's generation, and his recognition is overdue. Ernesto is delighted. Just the day before I'd gotten this note in English from Rivas: "As 'the last of the great American Christian drinkers'—I'm recovering from a Kerouac-Scott

Solentiname

Fitzgerald-Malcolm Lowry binge. My friends Kenneth Silverman and Bill Finnegan came to see me last night and now have this brief letter for you as a hail-farewell: *Ave atque Vale!*")

It's sunny outside. The roter blades whir with a singing sound, the motor drowning it out. We pass over Apoyo *laguna*, the crater lake, then Granada, and head out over Lake Nicaragua and islets we visited by boat Sunday. I am sitting in the doorway of the cockpit. The pilot has the map in his lap. Then we're passing Ometépé on the starboard, its two volcanoes wreathed in cumulus and hot-looking clouds . . . In a little over an hour we're coming in low over the so green hills of a little tropical island. It looks wild. We circle the end of it and come in over the lush treetops to land without a jolt in a bright green field, beyond a savagery of palms. Suddenly we've dropped into a lost tropic. Animals graze in the trees, bird-song lightens the air, a horse and rider pause to watch us. There are a few small white houses close by on a hill, and Ernesto's church. It is as if innocence itself in the shape of an island existed here still in a "sea of evil." That is the Romantic interpretation, the vision of the "noble savage" (debunked by modern anthropology), the idea of innocence echoing through time from the Desert Fathers to Rousseau. Somoza obviously thought otherwise. Ernesto was condemned to death *in absentia* for having been the planner of Solentiname and its (pro-Sandinist) community. It was some time in these days that Ernesto renounced the pure Gandhian principles of non-violence he had embraced with Merton. "Gandhi couldn't have stopped Hitler," he told me.

Some *campesinos* in straw hats are standing around watching us come across the meadows from the copter. There's a couple working on a new school building made of cinder blocks—no more than a room or two. An old *campesino* offers me his horse, and I gallop around the meadow. But Ernesto is impatient to tour the place with us. (He seems liberated, takes off his beret and puts on a *campesino's* straw hat.) Happily he shows us the restored church—a room of whitewashed simplicity. Above the altar a new cross has been erected, replacing the one made by Ernesto and destroyed by the *Guardia*. I ask Ernesto: "You don't say Mass these days?" "Only in private. And last New Year's here in Solentiname." The sunlight floods in. We are part of the primitive painting. But over the hill sits the copter.

Ernesto takes us around to see other projects underway. There is a toymaking and furniture shop, with new West German machines given by a German steelmakers union. There's a cultural center planned (by an Italian architect) on a little hillside by an inlet of the lake, so that the audience will look out on the lagoon . . . There's about a thousand people on the island, and there aren't any cars or trucks . . . About a dozen small deer graze in a large pen—for breeding. The community house has been rebuilt, and we sit out on its terrace. I go inside and see shelves of books; about 50 books make up the community library. There are five copies of Alvah Bessie's *Men & War*, and some texts in German. There's Ho Chi Minh and a manual of Marxism, upon which a hen is roosted. I hope it doesn't lay an egg.

A lunch is spread in the kitchen, and we have fish soup with beer. Ernesto tells me three boys in the former community died in the fighting (two captured alive and assassinated). Back on the porch, Ernesto shows me a photo book of the ruins of Solentiname, and one picture shows exactly the same scene as in a large oil painting I did just before leaving San Francisco which I had entitled "Nicaraguan Ruin."

Ernesto would like a little siesta, and he takes me across the hill to a new small house just finished for him, very plain, with single wooden beds, a desk and a bench. He has a TV. There is electricity. (Before Thomas Merton died in the Far East, Ernesto had built a small retreat for his master who had intended to visit here after his Far East trip.) There is also a new novices' house being built, very Spartan.

While Ernesto is trying to take his nap, a single gun goes off down the hill. Then another shot. Then another. Then another. (It turns out later that Ken Silverman had persuaded a soldier to let him try out his rifle. It was the only shot I heard fired in Nicaragua.) After a while we walk down to the pier where a long wooden skiff is tied up and an old rowboat is sunk. A couple of us swim way out, treading water out there while Ernesto strips to his underwear and bathes at the end of the pier, looking like the *Evangile* himself . . .

Back at the community house, we meet the captain in charge of the region (Rio Vista), and he tells us that 200 of Edén Pastora's men surrendered two days ago. There's still more than a thousand of them over there, he says, gesturing toward the Costa Rican shore. A couple of journalists from *La Barricada* arrive to interview him, and it's time for us to go.

Ernesto is staying overnight, and overjoyed he is to have a day off. He apologizes for not being able to see us off at the airport tomorrow. One of the last things he says to me, in answer to my question, is that it *is* possible to have "a civil libertarian Marxism." We part with an *abrazo*, and lift off in the late sun.

Everyone is pensive in the copter, looking back and down . . .

On the island, Ernesto had given me a copy of *Nostalgia del futuro: Pintura y buena noticia in Solentiname (1982)* in which he had written an inscription: "in Solentiname and also in the future . . . " It is filled with full-color reproductions of the primitive paintings done at Solentiname. I read from his Introduction:

I arrived in Solentiname with two other *compañeros* twelve years ago in order to found a small contemplative community. Contemplation means union with God. We quickly realized that union with God led us in the first place to union with the very poor and neglected peasants who lived scattered on the banks of the archipelago. Contemplation then led us to a political commitment: contemplation led us to revolution. It had to; otherwise, it would have been false. My old novice master, Thomas Merton, who was inspiration for and spiritual director of that foundation, had told me that in Latin America, a contemplative could not remain outside political struggles.

At first, we would have preferred a revolution based on nonviolent methods of struggle (even though we were aware of the Church's traditional principle of the just war, and the right of individuals and nations to legitimate defense). But later we began to realize that at present, nonviolent struggle is not practical in Nicaragua. Gandhi himself would agree with us.

Father Ernesto Cardenal in his restored chapel, Solentiname

Actually, all true revolutionaries prefer nonviolence to violence, but they don't always have the freedom to choose. What radicalized us most politically was the Gospel. Every Sunday at Mass we discussed the Gospel in dialogue with the peasants and they, with admirable simplicity and theological depth, began to understand the essence of the Gospel's message: the proclamation of the kingdom of God.

That's what this is: the establishment on earth of a just society, without exploiters or exploited, with all goods communally owned, like the society in which the first Christians lived. These discussions have been widely disseminated throughout the world in the book *The Gospel in Solentiname*, which has been translated into several languages. But above all, the Gospel taught us that the word of God was not only to be heard but to be put into practice.

And the peasants of Solentiname who studied the Gospel in depth could not help but feel solidarity with their brothers and sisters in other parts of the country who were suffering persecution and terror, who were imprisoned, tortured, assassinated, raped, whose ranches were burned, and who were thrown out of helicopters. They also felt solidarity with all those who were giving their lives for love of their neighbor. And for this solidarity to be real, one's safety and one's life must be risked. In Solentiname we knew that if we wanted to put the word of God into practice, we weren't always going to enjoy peace and tranquility. We knew the hour of sacrifice would arrive; and that hour arrived.

One day a group of young men and women from Solentiname (some from my community), because of their growing deep convictions, decided to take up arms. Why? They did it for one reason only: for love of the kingdom of God. Because of a fervent desire for social justice, for a real and concrete kingdom of God here on earth.

Down at the pier, Solentiname

When the time came, these young men and women fought with great courage, but they also fought in a Christian way. That one early morning in San Carlos, they repeatedly tried to reason with the army to avoid firing a single shot. But the army replied with machine guns and so, against their will, they also had to use their weapons.

I am pleased that these young Christians would fight without hatred, above all, without hatred for the soldiers, poor exploited peasants like themselves. It's terrible that there are dead and wounded. We wish there were no fighting in Nicaragua, but that doesn't depend on the oppressed people who are only defending themselves. Someday there will be no more war in Nicaragua, no more peasant soldiers killing other peasants, but instead there will be an abundance of schools, day care centers, hospitals and clinics for everyone, adequate food and shelter for everyone, art and recreation for everyone, and most importantly, love among everyone.

Translated by Barbara Paschke

Returned to Managua, it's our last night in Nicaragua, and after supper we are lucky to have a visit with two of the most important, if not *the* most important, men in the government: Daniel Ortega Saavedra (Miguel Cervantes Saavedra must have been a distant ancestor of his), the Coordinator of the National Directorate; and Father Miguel d'Escoto Brockmann, the Minister of Foreign Affairs. They drove to our house on their way to the airport to go to Venezuela. In contrast to Fidel Castro who gave me a very soft handshake when I met him in a restaurant in Havana in 1960,

Daniel Ortega gives me a much firmer one, but nothing macho about it, and he impresses me first off as another young intellectual whom I might have met in some graduate school in the States—nothing dictatorial or militarist about him, despite his immaculate uniform—another very good looking gentleman like Jaime Wheelock. (I am told he has two children with Rosario Murillo.)

We sit down in the old rocking chairs on the now dark veranda. Father d'Escoto is a Maryknoll priest, perhaps in his fifties, and went to UC Berkeley. His English is as good as any North American, and he comes to the aid of my Spanish from time to time, as we range over practically every subject already covered in this book. I feel an immediate affinity for both of them, and tell them I certainly agree with Eduardo Galeano's *Open Veins of Latin America* as an analysis of the imperialism which has bled Latin America for centuries, a thesis which doesn't need Marxist dialectics or Marxist ideology to prove. (I also mention the Grove Press book, *Dollars and Dictators*, published recently. They seem to be familiar with it.)

Daniel Ortega observes at one point that North American policy has *always* been one of "ignorance and arrogance." "American political behavior," he says "has been the same since the last century. That is the problem." But there is nothing belligerent or recalcitrant in his attitude; he added that he wished "America would *help* us make a *development model* in Nicaragua, to be used by all developing countries in which private and political sectors share in the problems." (These men don't talk like the militarist totalitarians I had been led to believe they were by the White House!)

Since our return to the States, the Sandinistas have announced politically free elections to be held this November, and it seemed in the conversation with these two leaders that this subject was uppermost in their minds, together with the constant apprehension that President Reagan might send forces to invade Nicaragua at any time. If only, they said, the U.S. would lay off, they might be able to have truly democratic elections. They were studying various models of government intently, and wished to come up with a model for "real democracy" in developing countries everywhere. I asked what of the British model, in which the Prime Minister's government falls whenever he can't muster a vote of confidence, so that the people aren't then stuck for years with an administration they don't support—as in the USA? Father d'Escoto laughed and said perhaps they needed a bit more stability than that at the moment. This wasn't England!

No it certainly wasn't England. (The ink on their Magna Carta isn't even dry. Or, some would say, it is still to be written.) And libertarian dissidents were still demanding that the Sandinista Front give up its political control of the army, of the police, and of the national television network, as well as end all press censorship, and abolish the military draft. Without this there could be no truly democratic free elections.

But, Daniel Ortega pointed out that at the moment the total effect of President Reagan's policies was to *impede* Nicaragua's progress toward any free elections and toward any kind of democratic Nicaragua. He also added that they fully expected, as soon as Reagan was re-elected, he would send the invasion forces.

We walked with them out to his jeep in the night after an hour or an hour and a half, shook hands warmly, and watched them drive away into the darkness of Nicaragua, wondering if we would ever see them alive again. Daniel Ortega was driving, with a young soldier next to him.

> We do not want that democracy where barely 30 per
>   cent of the population participates in electing its own
>   president;
> Here we do not want the democracy of the Ku Klux Klan.
> That kind of democracy we have already known, in the
>   times of Walker, in the times of Diaz and Moncada,
>   and in the times of Somoza.
> For us democracy is to truly love one another; which is
>   to say, to bury self-centeredness, greed, and the thirst
>   for gold.
> That is to say, to bury the exploiter and to raise the
>   exploited up out of their graves.
>   —*Daniel Ortega*

Comandante Daniel Ortega Saavedra (Right) driving away

February 2——At the airport early the next morning, two presents are delivered to us. One is a symbolic acrylic painting of paving stones used for barricades in the streets during the Sandinist uprising, sent by Rosario Murillo for the Sandinista Cultural Workers Association. The other is the painted wood head of a bull (with leather ears) mounted on a hoop skirt, used in traditional native dances. The name of the revolutionary bull is *El Toro Macho*.

The accompanying card is inscribed *"Daniel Ortega Saavedra, Comandante de la Revolución"* and is addressed to *"Compañero Lawrence Ferlinghetti."* *Campañero* is a word, one Sandinista told me, which avoids the connotations of the Communist Party "Comrade" (*Camarada*). To me it has always had a touch of the fields in it, of poor provinces, of the earth itself. The movement toward liberation by the *compañeros* and *compañeras* of the world, by the wretched of the earth, has been growing since before the French Revolution; and Nicaragua is a part of it. It is an irreversible revolution. *The past will not return.*

July 4, 1984